# OUR WORLD IN CRISIS

# GLOBAL POLLUTION

## RACHEL MINAY

**W**
**FRANKLIN WATTS**
LONDON•SYDNEY

Franklin Watts
First published in Great Britain in 2018 by The Watts Publishing Group
Copyright © The Watts Publishing Group, 2018

Produced for Franklin Watts by
White-Thomson Publishing Ltd
www.wtpub.co.uk

ISBN: 978 1 4451 6373 4

Credits
Series Editor: Izzi Howell
Series Designer: Couper Street Type Co.
Designer: Dan Prescott
Series Consultant: Philip Parker

The publisher would like to thank the following for permission to reproduce their pictures:
Alamy: Universal Art Archive 10b; Getty: Joe Traver 9t, Bettmann 9b, Hindustan Times 13t, Monty
Fresco / Stringer 13b, Stringer 15, Bloomberg 19t and 24b, YOSHIKAZU TSUNO/Staff 38; NASA:
image courtesy of Ozone Watch 17; Shutterstock: ssuaphotos *cover* and 6b, Fotos593 *title page* and
35, Tatiana Grozetskaya 4, Catarina Belova 5b, Burhan Bunardi 5t, J. Helgason 6t, Dmitry Birin
7, Denis Burdin 8, ChameleonsEye 10t, Joseph Sohm 11, Christopher PB 14t, MO_SES Premium
14b, Mary Terriberry 16t, paultarasenko 16b, Dmitriy Kuzmichev 18, Trueffelpix 19b, Gavin Baker
Photography 20, Ihor Bondarenko 21t, Becky Swora 21b, The Clay Machine Gun 22, gnomeandi
23, Aphelleon 24t, deb22 25, AVA Bitter 26, Ziablik 27, symbiot 28t, Jan Schneckenhaus 28b, chris
kolaczan 29, Asianet-Pakistan 30, FloridaStock 31, Rostislav Glinsky 33t, Monkey Business Images
33b, vchal 34, ShutterPNPhotography 36, littleny 37, Dizfoto 40, Olga Kashubin 41, SkyPics Studio
42–43, SamJonah 44t, AYA images 44b, John Gomez 45.

All design elements from Shutterstock.

Every attempt has been made to clear
copyright. Should there be any
inadvertent omission please apply
to the publisher for rectification.

Printed in China

Franklin Watts
An imprint of
Hachette Children's Group
Part of The Watts Publishing Group
Carmelite House
50 Victoria Embankment
London EC4Y 0DZ

An Hachette UK Company
www.hachette.co.uk
www.franklinwatts.co.uk

MIX
Paper from
responsible sources
FSC® C104740
FSC
www.fsc.org

# CONTENTS

# What is POLLUTION?

Planet Earth is amazing. It is unique in our solar system because the distance from the Sun, water on the surface and a breathable atmosphere all mean that it has the perfect conditions for life. But humans are creating more pollution than ever before and this is threatening the balance of our beautiful planet.

## What is pollution?

Pollution occurs when harmful or poisonous substances (called pollutants) damage the natural world. Pollution can affect the Earth's air (see pages 12–17), soil (see pages 18–19) and water (see pages 20–25). It can be solid, such as litter on the street; liquid, such as an oil spill; or a gas, such as pollutants from car exhausts or factory chimneys.

Emissions from factories and power stations are a major cause of air pollution.

## Sound and light

We usually think of pollution as something that makes the environment dirtier, but it can also relate to sound and light. Noise pollution – excessive noise – can be a problem for people who live near airports or flight paths. It also affects animals; for example dolphins and whales can be confused by the sounds from ship engines or submarines and become stranded.

Light pollution – too much artificial (usually outdoor) light – can be very harmful to nocturnal animals. Baby sea turtles hatch on beaches and use moonlight to know which way to crawl to the sea. Attracted and confused by artificial lights, they often wander inland where they can be eaten by predators or killed on roads. Bats usually leave their roosts to feed at dusk, when most insects are active. The more artificial light there is, the less likely they are to leave, which can have a huge effect on an entire bat colony. Birds that migrate at night and use the moon and stars to find their way are confused by the bright lights of cities, crashing into buildings or simply flying around until they are exhausted.

The world's cities are lit up at night. This doesn't just use vast amounts of electricity, but causes problems for wildlife, such as birds that navigate using the stars.

## Local and global

Local pollution affects the local area, for example litter dropped on your street or smoke from a neighbour's barbecue or bonfire. Other kinds of pollution can travel a long way, transported by wind, water courses and ocean currents. As the world's population increases and countries become more industrialised, pollution has become such a serious problem that it is affecting the whole planet. This is global pollution, and this book will show how we are all responsible for it and explore what we can do about it.

## What can you do?

The bad news is that we all contribute to global pollution. The good news is that means we can also all help to tackle it.

## What causes pollution?

Pollution can be caused naturally, for example by volcanic eruptions, wildfires and dust storms. Sometimes it is caused by accidents, such as a fire in a factory or a spill from an oil tanker. However, most pollution is caused by humans every single day. One major cause is burning fossil fuels such as coal and oil (see page 26) in power stations and vehicle engines; others are industries such as manufacturing, farming and mining. We all cause pollution and waste in our daily lives – using electricity, driving cars, buying things and then throwing them away.

A blast from a volcano causes air pollution, but daily human activity causes far more global pollution than volcanic activity.

## How does it affect people and wildlife?

Pollution can affect human health, for example polluted air can give people breathing problems. It can get into the food chain, where it affects not just one animal, but many – and also people who eat the polluted fish or meat. Litter, such as broken glass, can damage land animals, while plastic waste in the sea can entangle or suffocate marine animals and birds.

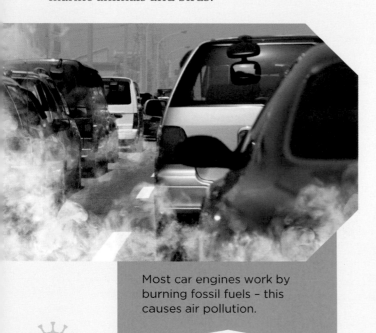

Most car engines work by burning fossil fuels – this causes air pollution.

On a global scale, there is very strong evidence that burning fossil fuels is causing global warming and climate change. What these words mean and what the effects are will be explored later in the book (see pages 26–31), but one example is how changes in the Earth's temperature affect wildlife. For instance, some animals migrate earlier or change locations entirely, which upsets the ecosystem and may mean that some animals die out completely.

## How long does it last?

Some kinds of pollution (for example bonfire smoke) do not last very long. The exhaust fumes caused by one car might not seem a lot, but the combined fumes from heavy traffic on a busy road will be much more damaging. Contamination caused by industry or by an accident such as an oil spill can stay in the soil for a long time. Radioactive waste, a by-product of nuclear power (see page 38), is extremely dangerous for thousands of years and needs to be stored very carefully, such as in concrete or stainless steel, and buried deep underground. At its worst, pollution can have devastating and long-lasting effects.

# CASE STUDY

### The Chernobyl disaster

Chernobyl was a nuclear power plant in what is now Ukraine. In 1986, there was a huge explosion in one of the four reactors. The fire that followed burned for nine days and winds carried vast amounts of radioactive waste over a wide area of Europe. More than 300,000 people had to leave their homes, 28 emergency workers died from acute radiation sickness and subsequent deaths from cancer have also been linked to the accident. An area of 2,600 km$^2$ surrounding the disaster site is known as the Chernobyl Exclusion Zone; no one is legally allowed to live there. The reactor was covered in a huge concrete 'sarcophagus' (another word for a coffin) to seal in the waste soon after the disaster; a new structure was begun in 2007.

The original 'sarcophagus' was only designed to work for 30 years. The new structure aims to contain the radiation for the next 100 years.

Although humans have always created some waste and pollution, people didn't think it was a problem until just over 50 years ago. So why did people's attitudes start to change?

### An ancient problem

Even in the distant past, people made pollution. It is thought that large-scale farming and burning wood to make metal weapons increased levels of a gas called methane in ancient Rome and China.

### The Industrial Revolution

Pollution increases with industrialisation and rising population levels. The Industrial Revolution began in Britain in the late eighteenth century. It led to greater production and wealth, but the smoke produced by burning coal in factories and homes caused breathing problems, and polluted water led to the spread of diseases such as cholera and typhoid. In the twentieth century, a number of specific cases indicated that pollution was becoming a serious problem.

Methane is a gas that contributes to global warming today. But how do scientists know there was methane in ancient times? They found bubbles of the gas trapped in ice that built up in Greenland over 115,000 years.

# CASE STUDY

### Love Canal, Niagara Falls, USA

From the 1920s to the 1940s, city waste and toxic chemical waste were dumped into an unused canal in Niagara Falls. In 1953, the Hooker Chemical Company filled the canal in and sold it to the city for just one dollar. Houses and a school were built on the site, but by the 1970s, poisonous waste was oozing up into backyards and the people living there reported serious health problems. The government declared an environmental emergency and Love Canal was abandoned.

This photo from 1980 shows a family sitting outside a boarded-up house after hearing that people have to leave Love Canal due to contamination.

# CASE STUDY

### Minimata, Japan

In 1956, people living around Minimata Bay in Japan suddenly started to get very sick and die. It was discovered that they were suffering from mercury poisoning. A local chemical plant had dumped waste, containing mercury, into the bay. Fish and shellfish absorbed the mercury and people became ill when they ate the contaminated fish. Over a thousand people died from what became known as Minimata disease.

This picture shows a fire on the Cuyahoga in 1952.

# CASE STUDY

### Cuyahoga River, Cleveland, USA

A river is made of water, so it can't catch fire ... can it? In 1969, the Cuyahoga River was so polluted with oil and rubbish that this is exactly what happened! Amazingly, this wasn't even unusual. But the 1969 fire marked a turning point – people realised they needed to act to prevent environmental disasters like this.

## The environmental movement

For many years, people were not very worried about the effects of pollution, but concern grew as pollution became worse. A protest movement began in the 1960s as people became more aware of environmental issues, and governments started to take action in the 1970s. Some of the major environmental organisations were started during this period, including WWF or the World Wildlife Fund (founded 1961), Friends of the Earth (founded 1969) and Greenpeace (founded 1971).

*Rainbow Warrior* is a ship that Greenpeace has used in many campaigns, including those against the dumping of nuclear waste.

# CASE STUDY

### Rachel Carson's *Silent Spring*

One of the things that sparked the environmental movement was a book published in 1962. In *Silent Spring*, the American scientist Rachel Carson described how pesticides used in farming – and in particular a pesticide called DDT – damaged the natural environment by building up in the food chain (see diagram). Carson's book raised public awareness and led to a ban on DDT in the USA in 1972.

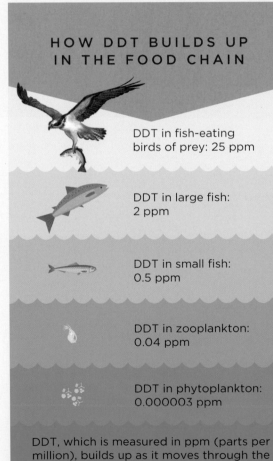

## HOW DDT BUILDS UP IN THE FOOD CHAIN

DDT in fish-eating birds of prey: 25 ppm

DDT in large fish: 2 ppm

DDT in small fish: 0.5 ppm

DDT in zooplankton: 0.04 ppm

DDT in phytoplankton: 0.000003 ppm

DDT, which is measured in ppm (parts per million), builds up as it moves through the food chain. It severely reduces the number of birds of prey (at the top of the food chain) by making the shells of their eggs very thin and breakable.

## What is sustainability?

Sustainability means not using resources that cannot be replaced, nor producing more waste than we can get rid of. We now know the way people lived in the past was not sustainable and has had a significant effect on pollution and climate around the world.

## Where are we now?

Unfortunately, we are still not living sustainably. Resources we have relied on for years are running out. While there are some people who do not believe that global warming is a threat, most scientists agree that human activity is polluting Earth's precious air, soil and water, and this is leading to climate change.

Many people care strongly about environmental issues and continue to work to raise awareness. In 2004, Kenyan environmentalist Wangari Maathai received the Nobel Peace Prize for her work with the Green Belt Movement, an organisation that encourages communities, particularly women, to conserve the environment. In 2006, the film *An Inconvenient Truth* showed how former US vice president Al Gore has tried to raise awareness of global warming.

Wangari Maathai founded the Green Belt Movement, which led to the planting of over 30 million trees across Kenya.

## What can you do?

Find out more about the current work that Greenpeace (www.greenpeace.org.uk) and Friends of the Earth (www.foe.co.uk or www.foei.org) do. Have a look at the website of the Young People's Trust for the Environment (ypte.org.uk/learn), which aims to encourage young people to understand the need for sustainability.

# AIR POLLUTION

All living things need clean air to survive, but pollutants in the air can damage the planet and human health. Vehicle use, industry and power stations create air pollution every single day. Huge environmental disasters – though rare – can also have devastating effects.

## Why we need clean air

Air contains nitrogen and oxygen, but also water vapour, carbon dioxide ($CO_2$) and other gases. Animals breathe in oxygen ($O_2$) and breathe out carbon dioxide; plants take in carbon dioxide and make oxygen – this is one reason plants are so important.

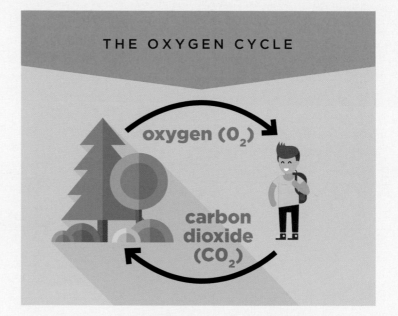

### THE OXYGEN CYCLE

oxygen ($O_2$)

carbon dioxide ($CO_2$)

## What is air pollution?

Air pollution is harmful gases or tiny particles in the air. The particles are often called particulate matter (PM), which means they are a mix of solid particles and liquid droplets. Although they are usually too small to see, they can be inhaled into the lungs and damage people's health.

## City smog

Cities are usually more polluted than the countryside. Smog (a dirty haze) is made when gases from industry and vehicles react with sunlight, and it can be a real problem in large cities. Vulnerable people – such as children, the elderly and those with breathing problems, for example asthma sufferers – are at particular risk from air pollution. In some cities, people wear masks to avoid the fumes and schools may restrict outdoor play or even close when pollution levels are very high.

All schools in Delhi, India's capital city, were shut for three days in November 2016 because the smog was so bad.

It was so hard to see during the London smog of 1952 that flares had to be used to guide vehicles.

## CASE STUDY

### London, UK

Can you imagine smog so thick that it actually blocks out the Sun? This is what happened in London in 1952. The smog was caused by soot ash and tar from burning coal in homes and factories, and it lasted for five days. Hundreds of thousands of Londoners suffered from stinging eyes and struggled to breathe. Thousands died. Four years later, the government passed the Clean Air Act, which banned the burning of polluting fuels in certain areas. This led to great improvements in air quality, but many people believe the problems caused by burning coal have now been replaced by those caused by traffic, in particular diesel cars.

## Transport

Vehicles, such as cars and aeroplanes, work by fuel being burned in the engine. This burning releases waste gases such as carbon dioxide, and poisonous gases such as carbon monoxide. Diesel cars are now thought to be particularly polluting, as they emit high levels of nitrogen dioxide and particulate matter (see page 12), both of which can cause serious health problems.

The governments of many developed countries (including the USA and Japan) have passed laws about cars and pollutants, and manufacturers have had to build less-polluting cars in response. Since 1993, all petrol cars sold in the European Union must have a catalytic converter fitted to the exhaust – this turns harmful pollutants into less harmful gases.

No one had a car 200 years ago. In 2010, the global number of vehicles exceeded 1 billion, which equates to one vehicle for 6.75 people worldwide. However, there are vast differences at country level, with the USA having a ratio of one car to every 1.3 people and India having a ratio of one car to 56.3 people.

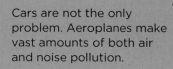

Cars are not the only problem. Aeroplanes make vast amounts of both air and noise pollution.

## Industry

Power stations make electricity by burning fossil fuels, such as coal or oil – this makes polluting waste gases. Coal-powered stations also create particulate matter. Nuclear power stations are one alternative to those that burn fossil fuels, but they carry their own risks and problems, such as deadly radioactive waste and terrible accidents (see also page 38).

Factories make waste chemicals that also pollute the air on a daily basis. In addition, industrial accidents can have catastrophic effects on human life and the environment.

# CASE STUDY

## The Bhopal disaster

In 1984, there was a leak at a pesticide plant in Bhopal, India. It blasted toxic gases into the local area where hundreds of thousands of people lived, many in slums. Thousands of people died instantly and in the days following; nearly 20,000 others are thought to have died since. Although the Bhopal disaster happened over 30 years ago, people are still campaigning for compensation and clean-up of the contamination.

Many thousands died as a result of the Bhopal disaster, while survivors lost their sight and suffered other health problems.

**What can you do?**

Try not to contribute to the air pollution that is caused by vehicles. Use cars less – walk or cycle for short journeys, which is healthier too! Use public transport, share cars or use car clubs.

## Acid rain

Another problem is that the polluting gases from factories and power stations mix with rain to make acid rain. This damages buildings and trees, and can kill fish and other animals in lakes and rivers. It is also an example of transboundary pollution, which means that it doesn't necessarily affect the countries that caused it, but can be carried by winds to nearby countries.

These trees in Virginia, USA, have been damaged by acid rain.

People have tried to tackle the problems caused by acid rain in different ways. Lakes and forests can be sprayed with lime to counter the effects of the acid, but this is expensive and it only lasts for a while. Many factory chimneys now have filters fitted that trap pollutants before they are released into the air. However, reducing air pollution overall is the only real solution to acid rain.

We all have to take steps to stay safe in the sun. The ozone layer works like sunscreen, so a thinner ozone layer means a greater risk of skin cancers.

## The ozone layer

Ozone is a gas. The ozone layer, which is high up in the Earth's atmosphere, helps protect us from harmful ultraviolet (UV) rays.

In the 1980s, it was found that the ozone layer was much thinner than it had been, especially over the Earth's polar regions. Something was damaging it – but what? Scientists discovered that the problem was CFCs, chemicals found in fridges, aerosol cans and foam packaging. As a result, governments in the 1980s worked together to ban CFCs.

Substances that damage ozone stay in the atmosphere for a very long time (around 40 years) so change is very slow, but the good news is they are now decreasing and the ozone 'hole' is finally recovering.

# CASE STUDY

## The Montreal Protocol

Two important international agreements helped to tackle the problem of the ozone layer – the Vienna Convention for the Protection of the Ozone Layer (1985) and the Montreal Protocol (1987), which specifically helped to ban CFCs. These two agreements were the first ever to be ratified (agreed) universally in the history of the United Nations (UN). They are an excellent example of how countries can work together to tackle global pollution and bring about environmental change.

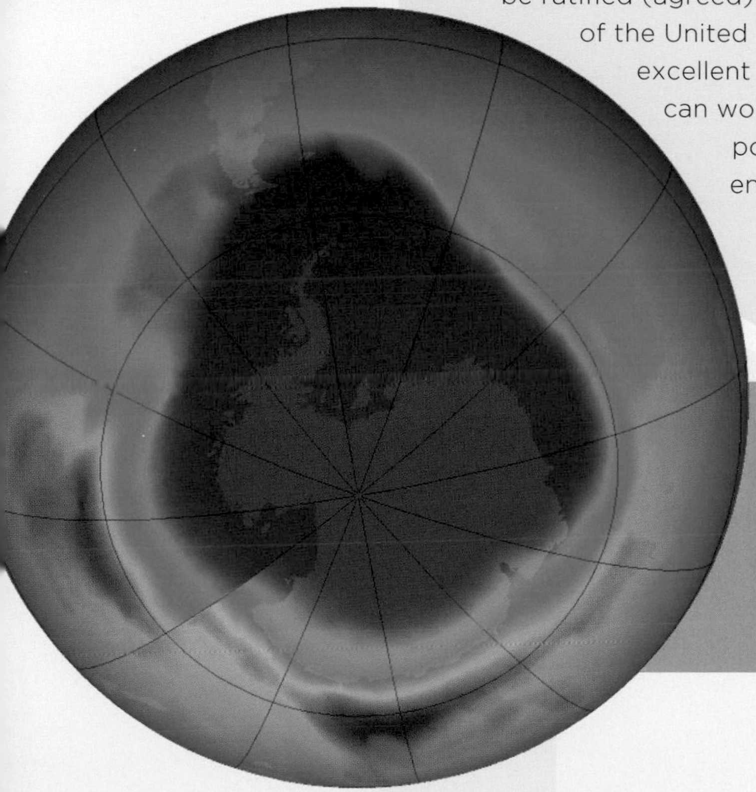

This picture shows the ozone 'hole' over Antarctica in 2012. Thanks to the Montreal Protocol, the concentration of the harmful substances that destroy ozone is now gradually getting smaller.

Soil is precious. Healthy soil helps plants grow well and makes more nutritious food for us to eat. However, this important resource can be polluted by industries such as mining, by the extraction of oil and gas, and by waste and sewage.

## Mining

Vast amounts of soil and rock are removed in mining operations, which build up as massive piles of waste. Chemicals used in the mining process, as well as pollutants from the waste itself, can seep into and contaminate the soil, before running off and polluting local rivers.

Surface mines, such as this coalmine, leave obvious scars on the natural landscape. Some people think this is a kind of pollution in itself.

## Oil

The oil industry is another major culprit of soil and water pollution. One of the most oil-polluted regions in the world is Ogoniland in the Niger delta.

# CASE STUDY

## Ogoniland, Nigeria

Shell (an oil and gas company) and the British government found oil in the Niger delta in 1956 – four years before Nigeria became independent from Britain. Numerous oil spills over 50 years made the soil across 1,000 sq km of Ogoniland heavily polluted and unsuitable for farming. The oil spills also contaminated rivers and drinking water. In 2011, a UN report said that clean-up would take 30 years.

This picture from 2016 shows a handful of the oil pollution caused by a damaged pumping station. Clean-up of Ogoniland was finally launched in the same year.

## Fracking

Fracking, or hydraulic fracturing, is a way of releasing oil and gas from a kind of rock called shale. It can be very controversial in the areas where companies want to carry it out, due to fears of soil, water, air and noise pollution, and potential triggering of earthquakes.

### THE FRACKING PROCESS

A high-pressure mixture of water, sand and chemicals is directed at the rock

Gas flows out

The rock fractures (breaks) apart, releasing the gas

## Waste and landfills

Waste is a problem whenever it is just dumped on the land, but it can even be a problem when people are trying to dispose of it properly. A lot of waste, including household waste, chemical waste and that left over from sewage treatment, is buried in pits called landfills (see page 34). The problem is that although landfills are supposed to be leak-proof, dangerous waste sometimes seeps into and pollutes the soil.

We share our planet with billions of animals and plants, and we all need clean water to survive. We also use water for washing and in industries such as farming, manufacturing, transport and making energy. However, the world already uses too much water, and polluted water sources threaten wildlife and human health.

### Agriculture

Much agriculture (farming) relies on the use of chemicals. Herbicides and pesticides are chemicals designed to kill weeds or pests that might damage or destroy crops. Fertilisers are designed to help plants grow. Chemicals used on the land sink into the soil and get washed into lakes and rivers.

### Fertilisers

Plants use nutrients in the soil to grow well. If the plants are left to die naturally, they decay back into the soil and the nutrients are replaced for the next generation of plants. However, when a farmer's crops are ripe, they are taken out of the soil – the nutrients cannot be returned and so the farmer adds nutrients in the form of chemical fertilisers. When these are washed into water sources, it causes a problem called eutrophication.

Farmers need good soil to grow strong and healthy crops, so it might be surprising that the agricultural industry has been one of the biggest causes of pollution.

The nutrients make a plant called algae grow strongly and cover the surface of the water.

↓

This blocks out sunlight, which kills underwater plants, resulting in less oxygen in the water.

↓

Bacteria feed on the dead plants, using up more oxygen.

↓

Fish and other organisms in the water die.

# CASE STUDY

### Lake Erie

At 388 km long and 92 km wide, Lake Erie is the fourth largest of North America's Great Lakes. The land around the lake is heavily developed with farms, cities, industries and sewage treatment plants. In the 1960s, Lake Erie was declared 'dead' due to eutrophication. Scientists discovered the cause was mainly phosphorus, a chemical that had got into the water via fertilisers and detergents. Because Lake Erie is bordered by both the USA and Canada, the two countries signed an agreement to improve water quality and this led to great recovery in the 1970s. However, conservation efforts were not kept up and the problems of eutrophication still persist today. Campaigners are fighting for funding to continue to protect the lake.

### Organic farming

Some farmers and gardeners choose to garden organically. This means not using chemical fertilisers, but using more natural methods such as manure to feed plants and rotating crops (growing them in different places each year) to make the best use of nutrients in the soil and avoid diseases. Organic farming produces lower yields (amounts of crops) than non-organic, but some scientists argue that more research could increase yields, while also bringing environmental and health benefits.

Although Lake Erie's problems are not solved, it represents how science, industry and governments can work together to bring about international change.

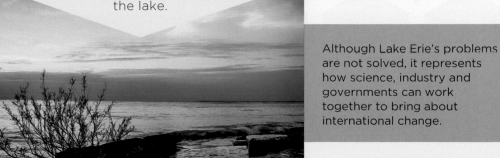

### Rivers

Power stations and factories use a lot of water, so are often built near rivers. Liquid waste from factories is sometimes poured directly into rivers, but this is now illegal in many countries. In some parts of the world, untreated sewage also enters rivers. Sewage makes algae grow more quickly, just as fertilisers do – so this also leads to oxygen being reduced in the water through eutrophication (see page 21).

People may throw rubbish directly into rivers and waterways. This not only looks horrible – it also poses a serious threat to wildlife and the environment.

### Thermal (heat) pollution

Factories use river water for cleaning, cooling and manufacturing. Thermal pollution occurs when warmer waste water is released back into the river. Warm water contains less oxygen than cold water and is also more likely to promote algae, and less oxygen in the water can kill fish and other organisms. Some organisms may die as a result of sudden temperature changes, while others may have problems reproducing or become more likely to catch diseases. Some species may be forced to migrate, changing the balance of the ecosystem.

# Water pollution

## Dirty water

We all have the right to clean water, but millions of the world's poorest people do not have access to safe water. According to the charity WaterAid:

- 663 million people live without safe water
- around 900 children under five die every day from diseases caused by dirty water and poor sanitation.

In some parts of the world, people have to trek long distances to fetch clean water. This job often falls to women and girls, which can affect their education and consequently their future lives.

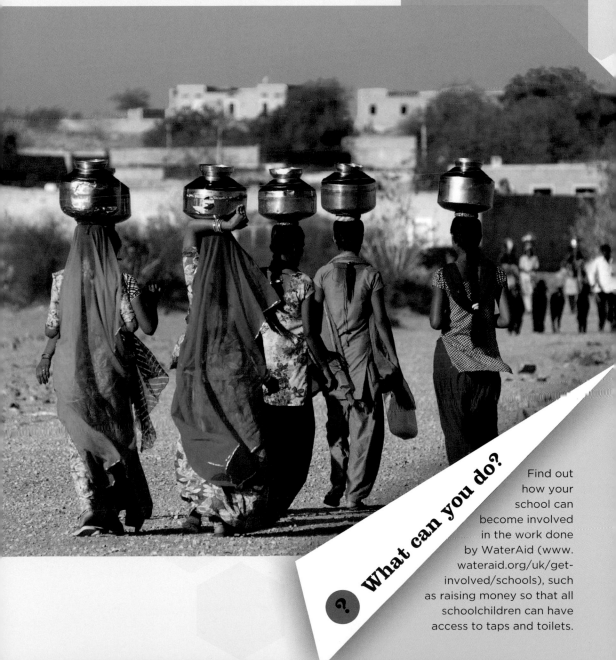

## What can you do?

Find out how your school can become involved in the work done by WaterAid (www.wateraid.org/uk/get-involved/schools), such as raising money so that all schoolchildren can have access to taps and toilets.

## Blue planet

Seas cover two-thirds of the Earth and 97 per cent of the planet's water is in the oceans. Our seas affect the weather, the land and the world's temperature, as well as providing food for billions of people. They are also a vital habitat – there may be as many as a million species of marine animals and plants.

## Polluting our seas

However, we need to protect the seas of our blue planet. Rivers drain into the oceans, carrying pollution with them. Pollutants, such as mercury, are particularly damaging because, like DDT, mercury builds up as it moves up the food chain. Raw sewage dumped in the sea, for example by cruise ships, carries bacteria that cause disease. Rubbish, chemicals and even radioactive waste are also dumped a long way out to sea, but currents and tides may spread the pollution far and wide. Accidents, such as oil spills, can have a catastrophic effect on wildlife.

The Deepwater Horizon spill is considered the worst environmental disaster in US history.

## CASE STUDY

### The Deepwater Horizon oil spill

The Deepwater Horizon was an oil-drilling rig in the Gulf of Mexico. In 2010, it exploded, killing 11 workers and leaking oil that flowed continuously for an incredible 87 days. The spill covered a vast 2,100 km of shoreline, causing the deaths of many thousands of birds, fish and sea creatures.

## Plastics

Plastic waste is also a massive problem in our seas. More than a million seabirds and 100,000 mammals and sea turtles die each year by getting tangled in or eating plastics.

Microbeads are tiny pieces of plastic used in cosmetic products. Some people think there may already be as many as 50 trillion microbeads in the world's oceans, where they harm marine life and can get into the food chain. However, this particular pollution problem has been a success story in terms of people power – so many people have put pressure on governments that a number of countries are now working to ban microbeads.

# CASE STUDY

## The Great Barrier Reef

Australia's Great Barrier Reef is the largest natural feature on Earth. It is formed of nearly 3,000 coral reefs and is home to millions of marine animals and plants. But the Great Barrier Reef is under threat from tourism and fishing methods, as well as from pollution and global warming. Healthy coral is colourful, but in recent years, warmer seas have been turning it white, indicating that the coral is dying.

Warmer waters killed off 22 per cent of the reef's coral in 2016; scientists are concerned that climate change is a huge threat to the future of this vital ecosystem.

## What can you do?

#2minutebeachclean is a movement that started in the UK but has spread around the globe. The idea is that if everyone spends just two minutes picking up litter every time they visit the beach, they can make a huge difference. Visit beachclean.net.

Find out more about microbeads and how to avoid them at www.beatthemicrobead.org.

So why are the seas of our blue planet getting warmer? The answer is to do with how we make and use energy, and the huge problems this can cause.

### Energy

Almost everything we do requires energy. We wake up in the morning and switch on a light, the radio or the kettle; have a hot shower; get a lift or catch a bus to school; use a phone, tablet or computer ... it goes on and on. Most of the energy we use – such as fuel for our cars or electricity – comes from burning fossil fuels.

How many energy-hungry gadgets does your family use each day?

### Fossil fuels

A fuel is something that can be burned to make energy. Coal, oil and natural gas are all fossil fuels. They are called 'fossil' fuels because they were made from the remains of dead organisms over millions of years. There are two serious problems with fossil fuels:

- We are using them up much faster than they can ever be made, so they will eventually run out.
- When burned, they release large amounts of carbon dioxide ($CO_2$), a major factor in the greenhouse effect and global warming.

## How a greenhouse works

Gardeners use a greenhouse because the air inside is warmer than it is outside. This is because heat from the Sun goes through the glass, but the glass traps some of it inside. Carbon dioxide is called a 'greenhouse gas' because it does a similar thing in the Earth's atmosphere – it stops all the heat from the Earth escaping into space.

## The greenhouse effect

A natural greenhouse effect is a good thing. In fact, it's what makes life on Earth possible, because without it the temperature would be around -18°C! However, very high levels of carbon dioxide, as well as other greenhouse gases (such as methane), trap too much heat, causing global warming.

### THE GREENHOUSE EFFECT

Solar energy from the Sun passes through the Earth's atmosphere

Some is reflected back into space

Earth's surface is heated by the Sun and radiates the heat back towards space

Greenhouse gases in the atmosphere trap some of the heat

## Scientists agree

Some people do not believe that human activity is causing global warming or even accept that it is really a problem. But the vast majority of scientists agree that humans are responsible for a dramatic increase in the greenhouse effect. In fact, most agree that temperatures are rising so much and so quickly, that it is threatening ecosystems and the future of our planet.

## What can you do?

? Be energy-wise! For starters, turn lights, computers and other gadgets off (don't leave them on standby), and turn the heating down. See pages 42–43 for more ideas.

## Meat and methane

Raising livestock for meat and dairy uses a lot of fertilisers, pesticides, animal feed and water. Livestock also make methane, a greenhouse gas. In fact, livestock produce around 15 per cent of the total greenhouse gases produced by human activity. What is more worrying is that this is increasing as the world's appetite for meat increases. From 1971 to 2010, the global population grew by around 80 per cent – that's a huge amount, but in the same period global meat production *tripled*. If this rate continues, methane will have an even greater impact on the greenhouse effect.

You might think increased meat production is a good thing – that it might solve the world's hunger problems – but probably the opposite is true. A meat-based diet uses up lots of resources, and a lot of land (about 30 per cent of the world's ice-free surface) is just used to grow animal feed. If some of this land was turned over to producing plant-based foods for people, it would be better for global hunger and global pollution.

Methane is produced by cows and other animals (including humans), growing rice and decomposing rubbish.

## Rainforests

Rainforests are some of the world's most amazing and important ecosystems – they contain about half of all the plant and animal species on Earth. They have also been called the 'lungs of the world', as they help us breathe by providing about a fifth of the world's oxygen and absorbing harmful carbon dioxide emissions.

Trees are vital for life and the health of our planet. Trees make oxygen and use up carbon dioxide, store carbon that could be harmful in the air, stop soil from wearing away and make food and homes for wildlife.

## Deforestation

In prehistoric times, forest covered more than half the land on the planet. But as populations grow and demand for wood increases, forests are being chopped down at a terrifying rate. According to the conservation organisation WWF, we're losing 33,000 sq km each year – or the equivalent of five football pitches every minute. Trees regrow, but they are being cut down far faster than they can ever grow back. What's more, fewer trees in the environment does not just mean a loss of habitat for wildlife, it means more carbon dioxide in the atmosphere, which fuels global warming.

# CASE STUDY

## Canadian tar sands

One energy project that has caused massive deforestation is the extraction of bitumen from areas known as 'tar sands' in Canada. Bitumen is a fossil fuel that can be used to make oil, and the Canadian tar sands produce an incredible 2.3 million barrels of oil a day. However, the process is very controversial because it is much dirtier than normal oil extraction and is thought to make three to four times more climate pollution.

The vast tar sands area in Alberta, Canada, was once important wetland and forest.

## What can you do?

Plant a tree! Avoid buying products made from new wood – buy second-hand where possible. If you do buy new wood or paper, check it comes from a sustainable forest.

## Global warming

So what does this all mean in terms of global warming? According to NASA:

- The global temperature has risen 0.8°C since 1880.
- 15 of the 16 warmest years on record have been since the year 2000.
- 2016 was the warmest year on record.

## Climate change

The difference between the words 'weather' and 'climate' is to do with time. The weather is whether it is rainy, sunny or snowing today, or over a short period of time. The climate is what the weather is like, on average, over a longer period of time. While 'global warming' means the rising temperature of the Earth's surface, 'climate change' means global warming and its effects, such as more extreme weather, species migrating earlier or moving altogether, ice in the polar regions melting and coral reefs dying.

Although the Earth has gone through several cycles of ice ages and different climates, most scientists agree that climate change has never been as fast or as extreme as it is at the moment and that this is caused by human activity, not as part of a natural cycle.

This picture shows some of the people affected by the 2010 Pakistan floods queuing for drinking water.

## Wild weather

In recent years, there have been more cases of extreme weather, such as record-breaking temperatures, floods, droughts and hurricanes. These can have devastating effects. In 2010, for example, severe flooding in Pakistan affected 18 million people, destroyed 12 million homes and polluted water sources.

## Rising sea levels

Sea levels have risen over the last century, and this has been at a faster rate over the most recent decades. This is a serious threat to coastal cities and low-lying countries such as Bangladesh and the Netherlands. There are two main reasons for this, both of which are connected to global warming. The first is that as the oceans warm up, they simply take up more space (because water expands as it heats up). The second is that rising temperatures mean that large areas of ice, such as those found in glaciers and at the North and South Poles, are melting fast.

Polar bears use ice platforms to hunt, so it is vital for their survival. Sadly, the loss of their habitat means polar bear populations are now in decline.

IF GLOBAL WARMING DOES NOT STOP

Sea levels rise by 18–59 cm by the end of the century

Stronger hurricanes

More droughts and floods

Less fresh water due to melting ice caps

More species migrating or dying out

More diseases such as malaria

# People and POLLUTION

It is not just people's activities, but the number of people that is the problem. The more of us there are, the more we need to take responsibility for our actions that are damaging the Earth.

## Population explosion

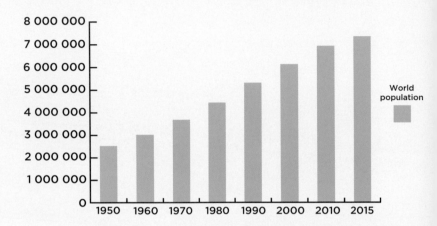

World population

This chart, based on data from the United Nations (UN), shows the dramatic rise in global population from 1950 to 2015. The UN predicts that in 2100 there will be 11.2 billion people in the world.

More people means more pollution, especially as countries become industrialised. More developed countries create a greater amount of pollution because they use more technology (and therefore electricity), and have more cars. On the other hand, developed countries should also have the money for technology that limits pollution. Less developed countries are industrialising fast, but may not have the money to do this in a less-polluting way. Wherever we live in the world, we need to use resources and energy more carefully.

## Consumerism

Consumerism basically means buying things in greater and greater amounts. Many people want the latest phone, games console or pair of trainers – and they want them now! But few people think about whether the company making the product looks after its workers or the environment of the country where it is made.

## Be a smart shopper

Consumers have a lot of power. If everyone stops buying a product because they don't like something about the way it is made, the manufacturer will soon realise they need to change. Ethical shopping is buying something that has been produced in a way that doesn't harm society or the environment, and there are loads of ways to be more ethical when you are shopping. For example, think about 'food miles' when your family is shopping for food – check labels in supermarkets to see how far something has travelled. If you can, buy local or even grow your own! Buy second-hand goods such as clothes, books or furniture; this avoids new things having to be made in a factory, which means not wasting resources or causing pollution – and it's cheaper.

Consumerism is an increasing problem in the developed world.

Buying locally is a great way to support smaller producers and avoid the pollution caused by air miles.

## What can you do?

Search YouTube for 'Kids & Consumerism' to learn more about consumerism from this video made by young people in the USA.

## Landfills

We don't just live in a consumer society – we live in a throwaway society. In the developed world, people buy vast amounts of stuff that is chucked away months, sometimes even minutes, later.

Most rubbish is buried in landfills. This might mean it is out of sight, but underground, some of it starts to decompose, releasing carbon dioxide and methane, both of which are greenhouse gases. When rain soaks through landfill, dangerous chemicals can also seep out into the ground.

## Incineration

Some rubbish is incinerated (burned), which means that it doesn't stay in the ground like landfill and can be used to make electricity. However, incineration releases air pollutants, including carbon dioxide, and burning rubbish that contains plastic can release poisonous fumes.

## Packaging

How often do you buy something, unwrap it and instantly throw all the packaging straight in the rubbish? In some houses, half of the rubbish thrown away is made up of packaging. It's true that not all packaging can be recycled, but the range of what we can recycle is growing all the time (see page 37). Packaging very often doesn't even serve a purpose – it is often only included to make a product look more appealing.

How much rubbish does your family throw away that will end up as landfill? Think about the rubbish all the families in your street, town or city and country create – this is why we all need to reduce waste.

## The plastic problem

Plastics are used in a vast range of products and they cause huge environmental problems both at the start and the end of their lives.

Plastic is made from oil, which is a fossil fuel. And when plastic is thrown away, although it might break up into smaller bits, it doesn't biodegrade (decay naturally). This is part of the reason it is such an issue in the world's oceans. Marine animals can consume small pieces of plastic by mistake, which can poison them or cause deadly blockages. Another issue is that these small pieces of plastic can also soak up pollution, which can then get into the food chain.

Think of all the plastic items you see around you every day. It's a scary thought that these will be in the environment for hundreds of years.

### TIME TAKEN TO DECOMPOSE

Paper, 2–4 weeks

Leaves, 1–3 months

Cotton, 1–5 months

Orange peel, 6 months

Drinks carton, 5 years

Plastic bag, 10–20 years

Aluminium can, 80–100 years

Plastic bottle, 450 years

Disposable nappy, 500–800 years

Glass bottle, 1 million years

## Reduce

So what's the best way to tackle waste? The answer is the three Rs – reduce, reuse, recycle. In the developed world, it can be very easy to think we want the latest technology or that we need new clothes just because we want a change, but every time we throw something away and a factory makes something new to replace it, it adds to the world's waste and pollution problems. Always think before you buy. Do you really need it? Will you use it?

The order of the three Rs is important! Reducing waste in the first place is the very best option. Reusing something is better than recycling it, but recycling is always better than disposing of something that will end up as landfill.

## Reuse

In the past, when things broke, someone fixed them. Now, in the developed world, people tend to throw the broken item away and just buy a new one. Before you throw away something you think is damaged or broken, find out if it can be fixed first. If something is fine, but you just don't want it anymore, give it to a charity shop or sell it at a carboot or school sale.

## Recycle

The table on the previous page shows that glass can take a million years to decompose naturally. The fact is glass should never be thrown away anyway, as it is one of the easiest materials to recycle. The range of materials that can be recycled depends on where you live, but is growing all the time.

# WHAT CAN BE RECYCLED?

Metals such as
food tins

Car batteries,
engine oil and tyres

Paper and
cardboard

Plastic bottles
and packaging

Batteries

Food waste

Garden waste

Glass

Electrical items such
as computers and
mobile phones

Liquids and
chemicals,
including paint

Textiles such
as clothing

Aluminium
foil

Always take a reusable
bag when you go
shopping and try to
choose products with
less or no packaging.

## What can you do?

Remember
the three Rs
and always try to
reduce the amount
of waste you make
first, then reuse, then
recycle as much as possible.
Challenge yourself to stop
as many things as possible
ending up buried in landfill sites.

We cannot undo all the harm that humans have done to the Earth so far, but we can all work together to find solutions. So what can we do to give our amazing planet a more sustainable future?

### Alternative energy sources

It would be great if everyone was more careful about the amount of energy they use, but it's not realistic to believe that people will be happy to live without electricity or give up their cars. However, we will *have* to rely less on fossil fuels in the future. So what are the alternatives?

### Nuclear power

Nuclear power is made by splitting apart atoms – the basic 'building blocks' of everything in the universe. People have very strong views about it. On the positive side, it is far less polluting than other ways of making electricity. In fact, many scientists and governments believe that it is the only solution to the desperate and urgent problems of climate change and fossil fuels. However, many others believe it is very wrong to rely on power that makes toxic radioactive waste, which cannot be dealt with safely and is so long-lasting. There is also always the risk of terrible nuclear accidents, such as Chernobyl in 1986 (see page 7) or Fukushima in 2011.

The biggest nuclear disaster since Chernobyl happened in Fukushima, Japan, in 2011. The nuclear power plant was damaged by a 15-metre-high tsunami that followed a devastating earthquake.

## Renewable energy

Renewable energy comes from sources that can be replaced and so will not run out. This is what makes them different from non-renewables, such as coal, oil and gas.

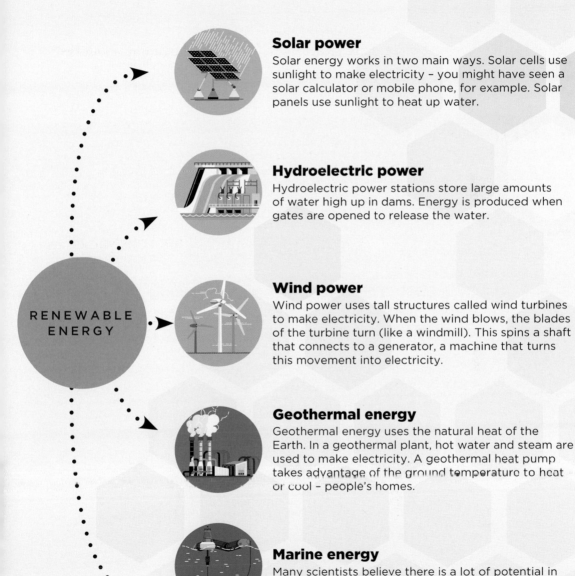

RENEWABLE ENERGY

### Solar power

Solar energy works in two main ways. Solar cells use sunlight to make electricity – you might have seen a solar calculator or mobile phone, for example. Solar panels use sunlight to heat up water.

### Hydroelectric power

Hydroelectric power stations store large amounts of water high up in dams. Energy is produced when gates are opened to release the water.

### Wind power

Wind power uses tall structures called wind turbines to make electricity. When the wind blows, the blades of the turbine turn (like a windmill). This spins a shaft that connects to a generator, a machine that turns this movement into electricity.

### Geothermal energy

Geothermal energy uses the natural heat of the Earth. In a geothermal plant, hot water and steam are used to make electricity. A geothermal heat pump takes advantage of the ground temperature to heat or cool – people's homes.

### Marine energy

Many scientists believe there is a lot of potential in the oceans to produce energy. Two ways that are already used are wave power – which harnesses the energy of the up-and-down movement of the waves – and tidal power, which uses structures similar to wind turbines, but underwater.

## What can governments do?

Governments can make laws to control pollution in their own countries and then ensure these laws are carried out. Of course, if the government of a country changes, this means that policies can also change – in the USA, for example, President Donald Trump reversed a number of climate change policies put in place by the former president, Barack Obama. The governments of different countries can also get together to make international agreements about tackling pollution, such as the Montreal Protocol to ban CFCs (see page 17) and the Kyoto Protocol to reduce greenhouse gas emissions.

## What can industry do?

The more polluting industries are working to clean up their acts, but there is always more that can be done. Factories are becoming cleaner – trapping dirt by filtering waste gases before they get out into the air. The vehicle industry has also made a number of changes, such as:

- making vehicles that run on natural gas, which makes less pollution than petrol
- making electric cars, which don't have an engine that burns petrol (although the electricity they use needs to be made at a power station)
- making hybrid cars, which have an electric motor and a small petrol engine, so make less pollution than a standard car.

Electric cars have batteries than can be recharged at points like this.

## What can science do?

Some scientists have suggested high-tech answers to global warming. One example is blasting massive mirrors into space that would not block out sunlight completely, but filter harmful UV rays. Another is firing clouds of sulphur into space to surround the planet and help cool it down. Other ideas relate to trapping and storing carbon dioxide or turning it into something more harmless, or growing more plants to soak it up.

## Sustainable technology

So far, these extreme solutions are just ideas and too expensive to be carried out. Scientists need to continue to research new technologies that help to protect, rather than damage, the environment. For development to be sustainable, it needs to help protect the environment, but also be affordable and have a positive impact on people's lives – otherwise people would not use it.

'Green skyscrapers' like this one in Sydney, Australia, could be one part of a solution to polluted cities. This is good for the planet – because plants use up $CO_2$ – but also makes a pleasant environment for the people living there.

## ? What can you do?

You can do a lot to help with the pollution problem by changing your own habits, but for massive global changes, governments need to be involved. If there is something you feel strongly about, write to your local politician or to the government of your country. You and everyone else can help by putting pressure on governments to make laws for change and – importantly – to see that they are then carried out.

## One person, big planet?

Problems such as global pollution can seem overwhelming and it can feel as though an individual person cannot make a difference.

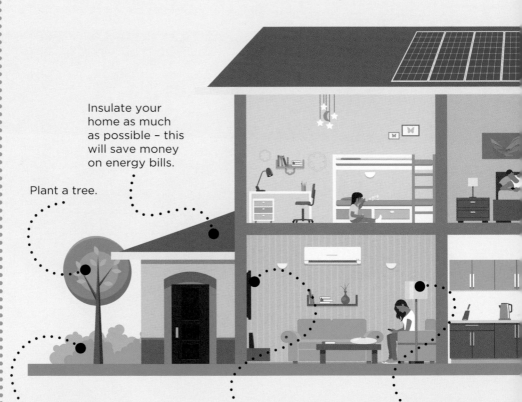

## LIVING MORE SUSTAINABLY

There are lots of ways people can live more sustainably. Not everyone can do all of these things, but the more you and your family can do, the better.

Insulate your home as much as possible – this will save money on energy bills.

Plant a tree.

Grow your own fruit and vegetables in a garden or allotment. You don't need a lot of space – herbs can be grown in a pot on the windowsill.

Turn appliances such as TVs and computers right off when they're not being used (don't just leave them on 'standby').

Use energy-saving lights and turn them off when they they're not being used.

But the fact is that the planet is made up of billions of individuals! We can all find out more about pollution and how to tackle it, work together to put pressure on governments and industries, and change our own everyday habits.

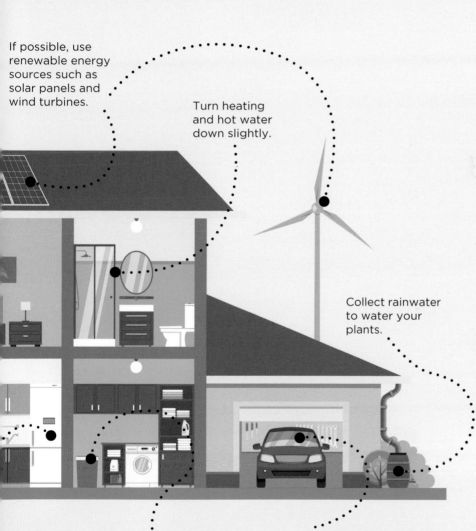

If possible, use renewable energy sources such as solar panels and wind turbines.

Turn heating and hot water down slightly.

Collect rainwater to water your plants.

Buy energy-efficient 'white goods' such as fridges and washing machines.

Think before you throw anything away that you know would go into landfill. Would someone else or a charity shop like it? Can it (or parts of it) be recycled?

Use your car less. Walk or cycle more, use public transport or share lifts with friends.

### Stick with it

It's one thing to know we should use less electricity, buy fewer new things, buy locally grown fruit and vegetables (or grow our own if we can) and walk or cycle rather than taking the car – but it's much harder to do it! What will you start with? Perhaps make a list of five things to change and stick it on a wall to remind you and your family. Then do it!

### Learn more

Follow the links in this book to find out more facts. It really helps when you are trying to change your own habits to understand and remember *why* you are changing them. Also, it makes it much easier to get other people to join you!

### Spread the word

Tell other people, such as your friends and family, about what you are doing and why it is so important to reduce global pollution. Can your family make bigger changes? Remind them that energy-saving ideas often save money, too.

An energy monitor is a great way to see how much energy your family is using and how much it costs. Go around your house turning things off to see how low you can get it!

People can grow their own food in allotments and community gardens, and even on rooftops. You don't need a garden – you can grow lots of things in pots in a yard, on a balcony or even on a windowsill.

What is your school doing? Can you get together with friends and talk to your headteacher or school governors about how you can make it greener? This could mean a big change like considering solar panels, but it could also mean a lot of smaller things such as reducing rubbish, growing vegetables or planting a tree.

Even if you are not old enough to vote, you can still make your voice heard! Get together with other people to raise awareness of local pollution problems and email or write to your local council about them. Contact the person who represents you in government (such as an MP) or write directly to the government of your country about the issues around global pollution that are important to you.

## For future generations

Remember that Earth is home to billions of animals and plants as well as to every one of us. It is our responsibility to do everything we can to make it clean, beautiful, healthy and safe – now and in the future.

Peaceful marches are a way for many people to tell governments what they think about important issues.

# GLOSSARY

**acid rain** – rain that has been made more acidic by mixing with air pollutants

**algae** – simple plants that grow in water

**biodegrade** – to decay naturally

**biodiversity** – the variety of plant and animal life in a particular area or habitat

**carbon dioxide** – a gas made when things are burned and which people and animals breathe out

**car club** – an arrangement where people share and can borrow a car

**climate change** – the rising temperature of the Earth's surface and its effects, such as melting ice caps and more extreme weather

**compensation** – money given to make up for loss or injury

**controversial** – likely to cause disagreement

**decompose** – rot or decay

**ecosystem** – all the animals and plants living in a particular environment

**emission** – something, such as gas, that is sent out or released (into the atmosphere)

**eutrophication** – when too many nutrients in water cause increased growth of plants such as algae, resulting in less oxygen in the water, which causes other organisms to die

**food chain** – a series of plants and animals, where each feeds on the one below it in the chain, for example: grass ➡ cow ➡ human

**fossil fuel** – a natural fuel, such as coal or gas, formed from the remains of living organisms millions of years ago

**genes** – the parts of living cells that inherit characteristics from parents

**global warming** – the rising temperature of the Earth's surface

**industrialised** – used to describe a country that has many industries (where things are produced in factories)

**landfill** – disposing of waste by burying it in a pit

**marine** – to do with the sea

**methane** – a gas produced by decaying matter and livestock

**migrate** – move from one area to another

**navigate** – to find the way to get somewhere

**nocturnal** – active at night

**nuclear power** – energy made in a nuclear power plant by splitting atoms apart

**nutrient** – a substance that helps things grow

**nutritious** – good for you

**pesticide** – a chemical used to kill pests such as insects

**pollutant** – a harmful or poisonous substance that damages the natural world

**reactor** – the part of a nuclear power station where the nuclear reaction takes place

**sustainability** – not using resources that cannot be replaced, nor producing more waste than we can get rid of

**transboundary pollution** – pollution that is made in one country, but travels by water or air to damage the environment in another country

**tsunami** – a long, high sea wave, often caused by an earthquake

**ultraviolet (UV) rays** – a type of radiation produced by the Sun

**United Nations (UN)** – an international organisation that works together to improve human rights and reduce wars

**urban** – to do with cities

# FURTHER INFORMATION

## Books

**Oil: Is it the Future of Energy? (Question it!)**
Philip Steele (Wayland, 2017)

**My Bed and Other Home Essentials (Well Made, Fair Trade)**
Helen Greathead (Franklin Watts, 2015)

**Pollution (Geography Detective Investigates)**
Jen Green (Wayland, 2009)

## Websites

Find out more about global pollution on these websites:

climatekids.nasa.gov
NASA's guide to the big questions around climate change and the environment

www.sciencemuseum.org.uk/climatechanging/climatescienceinfozone.aspx
Information about the science and future of Earth's climate from the
Science Museum in London

ypte.org.uk/factsheets/pollution
Pollution factsheet from YPTE (Young People's Trust for the Environment)

# INDEX

# OUR WORLD IN CRISIS

**W**
FRANKLIN WATTS
LONDON•SYDNEY